Pushing through the Pain

Dawn Wiedeman

India | USA | UK

Pushing Through the Pain © 2023 Dawn Wiedeman

All rights reserved.

No part of this publication may be reproduced, stored in a retrieval system, or transmitted, in any form or by any means, electronic, mechanical, photocopying, recording or otherwise, without the prior written permission of the presenters.

Dawn Wiedeman asserts the moral right to be identified as author of this work.

Presentation by *BookLeaf Publishing*

Web: www.bookleafpub.com

E-mail: info@bookleafpub.com

ISBN: 9789358367690

First edition 2023

I dedicate this book to anyone who has ever experienced pain at the hands of someone you love, may you know you are not alone and that growth is on the horizon.

ACKNOWLEDGEMENT

To my family and friends who always support my growth and creative spirit, I thank you!

PREFACE

Here's to the person just trying to fake it
Who put on a smile, just trying to make it.

Here's to the crier who got out of bed,
And the over-thinker who left things unsaid.

Here's to the fighter who didn't give up.
For the one who walked away when enough was enough.

Here's to the clown laughing their way through pain.
And the one who writes to keep themselves sane.

Here's to the heartbroken from a love that is lost,
Who put it all on the line, no matter the cost.

Here's to the scarred hearts and tear soaked faces,
For the baggage carried to unfamiliar places.

Here's to the walled in scaredies and the outgoing messes.
For the reassured moments and second guesses.

Pain is not something you have to face alone.
Nor is it a place your heart should call home.

I hope this helps you to heal and to grieve
And that happiness is a construct you now can conceive.

Seeping Out

Cracks now turn to craters,
My heart is seeping out,
The pain is taking over,
Not a single breath without.

I try to contain it.
Lock it up inside.
But the pain I am feeling, can't be faked,
Nor the solemnness denied.

Fake smiles make no difference.
They can't mask all I endure.
My eyes show the darkness,
Of my light burned out I'm sure.

I love with my whole heart.
I wear it right there on my sleeve.
Which makes the pain that much more unbearable,
When people choose to leave.

Stuck in this hell of thought,
This tower of misery.
Each painful thought plays on repeat,
Each painstaking memory.

I cry in the silence.
I smile in the light.
I pretend that I'm okay.
And that everything's alright.

I don't talk about the setbacks,
Or the heartaches over the years.
I just sit in my room alone,
Engulfed in covers and tears.

My silence means my hurt has consumed me,
No longer can I fake a smile.
You're just now seeing all that I carry,
Though I've been carrying it a while.

My thoughts are all consuming,
Each one escapes onto this page.
Trying to contain my pain,
Is quickly turning it to rage.

Why am I never enough?
Why don't they ever stay?
Why is the easier option
Always for them to walk away?

I could beat myself up,
And take all the blame.
But none of that would matter,
The result would be the same.

I would still have an ache in my chest,
And the sadness in my heart.
Wracking my brain for answers,
Picking all past words apart.

In my quest for understanding,
I keep checking my phone.
Only for nothing to be there,
And to still feel all alone.

So time to put it down,
And give up hope, I'm on their mind.
And realize the truth of the matter,
That again, I've been left behind.

The cracks now turn to craters,
My heart is seeping out.
The pain is taking over,
Not a single breath without.

Internal Flame

No matter how hard I try,
No one clicks like he did.
He loved not only me,
But also my kid.

From the moment we met,
He lit a spark in me.
Lit my world on fire,
For all the world to see.

But that flame I once had,
Is barely embers these days.
My heart is now darkness
Where there once was a blaze.

I've tried to get out there,
They say that's what people do.
Trying to find that spark,
An inferno for two.

I keep searching for "him",
And for my fire to ignite.
But it just isn't happening.
It just doesn't feel right.

No spark, no ember,
No glint of a flame.
Without him around,
My fire isn't the same.

I miss him. I love him.
I want the flame restored.
I want to make it work,
And overcome all we've endured.

No more searching for clicks,
Or matches that won't light.
I found him already,
My perfect Mr. Right.

And while it may burn
Getting too close to the fire.
Being with that man of my dreams,
Is my greatest desire.

Skip the Marriage

I skipped the marriage
Went straight for the divorce
Want a lesson on screwing things up
I'll give a crash course

No need to wait for the other shoe to drop
Self sabotage is a specialty of mine
Things can be perfectly perfect
A ring, the next thing in line.

Oh but wait here she comes.
The one woman destruction crew.
She will knock a hole in our plans
And the whole thing is through

But then I want it back
I've learned the error of my ways
But I just mess it up again
Just give it a few days

I guess I don't think I deserve it…
Love that is true
So I break my own heart in pieces
And then I blame you.

When will I learn
To stop breaking what's not broken
To leave a bit in the silence
To leave words left unspoken

To Stop searching for a problem
Where there isn't one
To Stop calling it quits
Before it is done

To learn The shoe isn't dropping
There is no trouble there
To stop putting myself through pain
And unwarranted despair.

I skipped the good parts
And lit a flame to happiness,
I should've seen this coming.
There were signs, I must confess.

He got too close,
Or that's the lie I like to tell.
For why I pushed him away,
Even after we both fell.

The shoe never dropped,
I threw it at myself.
I ruined everything,
Despite the love I felt.

I didn't want it to end
But it ended anyway.
I know I am the reason
He decided not to stay.

I can't hide behind the truth;
I'M the one who confirmed my fears.
No one to blame but myself,
I'M the reason for my tears,

I let fear guide me
Down a dark and painful road
One where my worries lead the way
And left my truths untold

This path of self destruction
Is one I can't continue on
One day I'll have to let someone in
To see the real Dawn.

But for now the walls are up
My armor is in tact
Because my heart is broken
Lost loves last impact.

So protection will be more
My walls now reinforced
I guess we'll see what life has in store
When I allow love to run its course.

Deep Breaths

Deep breath in
It will be okay
Deep breath out
He won't walk away.

Breathing getting rapid
I can't seem to calm myself.
the happiness seen in this house
Are now just the pictures on the shelf.

I thought we could work it out
I thought he would see my side
But instead he walked away
And I sat still and cried.

Deep breath in
This is only temporary
Deep breath out
Oh; quite the contrary

He left and isn't coming back
His things have all moved out
I thought he would stay and fight
But he just left without.

Without a care for my feelings
Or the pain he left behind
Without leaving even an ounce of hope
Or simple peace of mind.

I thought we were worth more,
He said he'd love me his whole life
I guess the day will never come
Where he'll make me his wife.

A simple argument turned ugly,
You said that we were through
You said that you would never leave
And I naively trusted you.

Deep breath in
This isn't real. He'll come back.
Deep breath out
You silly girl. You sat and watched him pack.

The suitcases are all gone now,
Not a trace that he was here.
No one left for you to cuddle with
Or to comfort you my dear.

But hold your head up now.
You're worth more than what he gave.
You can't fight to reclaim something
That isn't worth the save.

You saw the happy picture,
The future seemed so bright.
But in the blink of an eye that dream
Was gone and out of sight.

So have your cry
Or stay in bed awhile.
Because one day you'll find someone
Who will return your pretty smile.

One day you'll find the man
Who will fight tooth and nail for you,
The one in God's plan
A man who's worthy and true.

Take your time to heal sweet girl
There is no race to be won,
For the perfect man will wait for you
Until your healing is done.

Deep breath in
Healing is just around the bend
Deep breath out
The pain and suffering is coming to an end.

From Peace to Pieces

You found me at peace
But left me in pieces
My fortitude declines
My astonishment Increases

How could you love someone so much
And then pretend that doesn't matter.
Were all those words you said
Meant to reel me in and flatter?

I won't believe it was all fake,
I can't fathom it wasn't real.
I won't suppress all my memories
Because you can't fake the love I feel.

How can you just turn it off?
How can you lock it all away?
Why won't you show emotions?
I can't stand your stoic way!

I was fine before I met you
Perfectly content with just getting by
But then you turned my world on it's axis
Now all I do is cry.

I wake up puffy faced,
Nose stuffed from all the tears.
You said you wouldn't leave me
But instead confirmed all my fears.

You broke the deepest parts of me
The ones I never let come out
Where you were to be my comfort
You left me with self doubt.

You once picked up the pieces
And put them back together
You said I was the one for you
and that we'd be forever

But the pieces are more shattered now
Because I let you in
I have no more fight in me
I give up. You win.

You found me at peace
But left me in pieces.
The pain one man can cause
truly never ceases

The Truth of the Matter

Some days I'm "fine"
Others a complete mess
Some days I can bare it more
Others a little less.

I try to smile
And put on a brave face,
But the truth of the matter
Is tears want to take its place.

Faking happiness is a task
That gets harder everyday
I try to put on a front
But emotions get in the way.

The truth is that I'm broken
My insides torn to pieces
The "togetherness" I display
Is brokenness hidden in the creases

I've got a heart full of stitches
Trying desperately to mend
Searching for a place to be myself,
And no longer play pretend.

Where the walls can crumble
And the real me can come out.
Where my mind is filled with hope
And no longer with self doubt.

Where I can be seen
And my words validated
Where my emotions are not overlooked
Or merely placated.

I want to stand in the sunlight
and let the real me shine through.
I don't want to simply exist
But to thrive and feel renewed.

I want my truth to be visible
And not hidden in the dark
I want to move forward in my life
And not be stuck in park.

The truth of the matter
Is that the struggle is real.
And that this pain is unbearable
And at times not ideal.

The truth of the matter
Is that getting out of bed is sometimes hard
And that my pain can't be fixed
With a simple sympathy card.

So I take a deep breath
And push the pain down a bit more
And hope that someday soon
My faith can be restored.

Dating App

I put myself out there.
I joined the dating app.
They said they were looking for love,
 But that was a cap.

Dating in your thirties
Is like a used car lot.
You come for a trade in,
But leave with what you got.

It's almost better to stay alone
Then waste your time with these clowns.
Who are full of lip service
And countless let downs.

Communications are limited
To emojis and sex.
Is it too much to ask,
For a conversation that's complex?

I don't care what you drive,
Or how much money you make.
I don't care "what you're packing"
As I'm sure the picture is fake.

I don't need love at first sight.
The wedding can wait.
But I want more than a one night stand
Or a forgotten dinner date.

Time to delete these apps.
Dating is lame.
I guess I'm a free spirit.
Too wild for one man to tame.

Worth the Fight

My life is a little dark.
I'm starting to mind it.
I'm looking for the light.
But I just can't seem to find it.

I look for the rainbows
But all I see is rain.
Trying to find the lightness
Through all of this pain.

Another day.
Another fake smile.
Another heartbreak.
Another denial.

I thought this would be different.
I thought THIS was finally it.
I thought he would fight for me,
But instead, he just quit.

I am worth the effort.
I am worth the fight.
I am worth the response.
I am worth the goodnight.

But I guess he didn't think so.
With how easily he walked away.
I'm all out of fight,
I won't beg him to stay.

The days get darker
The thoughts like to creep in.
My mind is viciously whirling.
Why am I not worth keeping?

I let down my guard.
I gave him my heart,
I gave every piece,
Not just a part.

But it wasn't enough,
It wasn't meant to be.
I've opened my eyes now.
I'm starting to see.

The problem wasn't me.
I've done nothing wrong.
He wasn't my person.
Which I think I've known all along.

He is no longer worth my time,
Nor the effort that I gave.
This isn't a relationship
That is worthy to save.

I kept trying to make it work.
A square piece in a round hole.
But it just wasn't right.
I knew it in my soul.

Time to dry the tears,
And hold my head high.
Realizing the best thing for me
Is to finally say goodbye.

Questions

I ask myself why you left.
Why you didn't stay and fight.
The thoughts of the "whys" whirling
Keep me up at night.

In a fit of rage,
I yelled with "no regret"
But when the morning came around
I wished I could forget.

I wished I hadn't been half asleep
When I hung up on you
I wished I hadn't shouted in anger.
"If you leave, we are through!"

I replay the harsh words,
The actions that led to our demise,
And I wished you would've come back,
To see the pain left in my eyes.

I think about the moments
When my heart broke right in two
As I saw you walk away that night.
No more "me and you".

I wonder if I'd tell you how much your actions hurt?
Or if I'd hold that thought inside?
Would I continue showing my emotions
Or would I instead lead with my pride?

Would I stand there in silence,
A plain look on my face?
Or would I lay out all the facts,
And state my painful case?

It really doesn't matter now,
What the answers truly are.
Because the answers change nothing,
The anger took it too far.

There's no coming back from this.
I know the trust has gone away.
Because no matter what we want,
We don't both feel it's safe to stay.

You think I've left a door open,
You're afraid that I will leave.
But you're the one who keeps leaving,
That's the part I can't conceive.

Now you spend your time with others,
Knowing how it makes me feel.
I don't understand your actions.
And it makes me question what was real.

I have so many questions in fact,
But the result is still the same
Our journey has sadly ended,
And we are BOTH to blame.

So while the questions remain
and the healing will be slow,
I know I must convince myself
It is time to let you go.

Wish You the Best

You've taught me a lot,
The breakup taught me more.
I know that I am worthy.
And that I'm worth fighting for.

So I wish you the best
For whatever is to come
I hope you get all that you deserve….
And then some.

I pray the woman of your dreams
Brings out the best in you.
I pray you work together
In everything you do.

I pray you Don't speak in anger
Or make decisions you'll regret
I pray you're quick to forgive
And even quicker to forget

I pray that when you find her
That your smile will be real
That you won't hold my faults against her.
And you'll tell her how you feel.

I pray that you find peace in her eyes
And comfort in her touch.
I pray all this and more for you
Because I love you so much

While our story has ended,
Doesn't mean we won't find love
For it is written in the stars
By our author from above.

I'm thankful for the lessons,
The smiles and the laughter,
So here's to you and your future
With happily ever after.

Weeping Sky

The sky is weeping,
But I am not.
My head is spinning.
I am deep in thought.

The house is empty,
As I lay in bed.
I should be sleeping
But I'm thinking instead.

The lightning strikes,
And then the thunder.
My mind is ablaze,
With curiosity and wonder.

The day's tasks dance around,
I'm unable to sleep.
I stare up at the ceiling,
My thoughts getting deep.

I think back to the days
That have long since passed now,
Thinking about it all,
The who, what, when, where, HOW???

How did we get here?
This place of desolation.
Clouded and void of love,
Full of so much isolation.

Why am I here alone?
When we once were side by side.
Was it actions of anger?
Or someone's foolish pride?

The thoughts are spinning
With no sight of slowing down.
When I start to think I've got it
The thoughts go round and round.

I thought I put them to rest,
I thought I had found some peace.
But the calmness in my heart
Was just my eyes release.

Tears are now falling,
So much confusion and pain.
My thoughts are viciously pounding
Like this unrelenting rain.

Whirling winds and cracking limbs,
The trees break like my heart.
I don't know what to think anymore,
My insides break apart.

Lost in thought and confusion,
Curling tightly in my bed,
There is pounding on my window,
But even more inside my head.

Confusion is an understatement,
Why can't I figure this out,
Why is my mind filled with questions,
And considerable self doubt?

Why can't I figure out what I'm thinking,
Why do I have so much back and forth,
Why can't I get on the right path,
And find my true north?

Saying Sorry is Hard

Saying sorry is hard
Saying goodbye is harder.
I asked for communication
Because without is a nonstarter.

If I can't trust you,
And you wont trust me
Then what are we doing here?
Just a game of wait and see?

I'm too old for mistreatment
Too old for all the lies.
If you can't say you're sorry
Then it is time for our goodbyes.

I don't want to keep going round and round
There is no point in this game
Whether it is today or tomorrow
The result will be the same

I won't live a life where I'm left in the dark.
I need you to be open with your words.
I need to know what you're thinking.
I don't think my requests are absurd.

I need you to spell it out.
I don't want to guess how you feel and be wrong.
I need to HEAR the words.
Not read a text or listen to it in a song.

An apology alone won't solve our problems.
We have a lot to discuss for sure.
But I need to know that you are in this,
And that your intentions are pure.

I need to know that if I put in the effort,
That I'm not alone in this fight.
I need to know I won't be left with questions
That will keep me up at night.

Saying sorry is hard.
Saying goodbye is harder.
I refuse to be alone in this
And be this love story's martyr.

I don't want this to end
But I can't do this alone
And I can tell you're annoyed
By your words and your tone

So I'll leave you be now
You know where to find me
I won't keep reaching out
Those days are behind me.

If you want this to work
Then it's your turn to try
I've done all I can
To win back my guy.

So if this is the end
I wish you the best
On all your adventures
And future loves quest.

But I give you this advice,
Take it if you will.
Honesty and communication,
Are truly a big deal.

So good luck and goodbye.
If this is truly it.
I gave you my heart,
Every single bit.

On the Hook

You don't really want me
You just want me on the hook
If someone new came along
You wouldn't give me another look

You treat me like an option
But it's time I use my voice
I won't keep doing this.
I'm NO second choice.

I see it clearly now.
We're just not the same.
I'm in it for the long hall,
While you're playing a game.

I deserve to be chosen.
Day in and day out.
I deserve to be reassured.
Not left with self doubt.

I deserve the world.
Not just the part you choose to share.
I'm not like the others.
A heart like mine is rare.

It's so obvious now,
We're not on the same page.
While I want to connect,
You want to disengage.

You're out the door
And I'm here all alone
So It's time to move on
And delete you from my phone

Tonight is the perfect time,
To start putting myself first.
I gave you my best.
While You gave me your worst.

No need to gaslight me further.
Your silence said enough.
I won't lie and say I'll be fine,
I know this'll be tough!

But I know that THIS isn't it.
I deserve more than this.
So no more strife for me.
I'm headed to find my bliss.

I'm done listening to the silence,
Or the lies that you fed me.
I have only one regret….
That it took me this long to see.

Enjoy a life void of my presence
and the true love I gave
Because the hurt you caused
Sent my heart to its protective cave

You won't be seeing the real me
That I shared before
So enjoy the "greener grass"
Because you and I are no more.

Its Hard... It's Even Harder

It's hard to remember to do things for me.
It's harder to get out of the fantasy.

It's hard not to hold on to the past.
It's harder to see you move on so fast.

It's hard to look at you some days.
It's harder to move to the next phase.

It's hard to see through the pain.
It's harder to taper my disdain.

It's hard to feel like this all the time.
It's harder to continue to ignore the sign.

It's hard to think through all the things.
It's harder to not have the wedding rings.

It's hard to know what I know now.
It's hard to have believed that vow.

It's hard to wonder how I couldn't see.
It's harder to have believed this fallacy.

It's hard to see with clear eyes.
It's harder to have been fooled by your disguise.

It's hard to put a smile on my face.
It's harder to not feel safe in this space.

It's hard to trust you with any bit of my heart.
It's harder to not fall completely apart.

It's hard to have so many feelings alone.
It's harder to no longer feel like you're home.

It's hard to wake up and you not be in bed.
It's harder to believe a single word you said.

It's hard to not bite my nails 'til they bleed.
It's harder to no longer be someone you need.

It's hard to say all the things I need to.
It's even harder not to want to call you.

It's hard to keep it all bottled up inside.
It's even harder to swallow my pride.

It's hard to push forward and move on.
It's even harder to realize you're long since gone.

It's hard to stop the spinning round.
It's even harder to try and stand my ground.

It's hard to let you go and to heal.
It's even harder to believe any part of this is real.

I've Been

I've opened up fully. I've shown every part.
You can find it on my sleeves, my sweet battered heart.

I've stood nice and tall. I've fallen to my knees.
I've locked away my heart, and thrown away the keys.

I've been strong. And I've been weak.
I've talked a lot, and been unable to speak.

I have stumbled. And I have fallen.
I've gone broke when I went all in.

I've been cheated, and I've been lied to.
I have laughed, and I have cried too.

I've had my heart stolen. And I've given it freely.
I've been open and I've shown the real me.

I've been protected and I've been guarded.
Love's been ended and it's been started.

I've been through tribulations and I've been through trials.
I've been through pain and pasted on smiles.

I've been lost and I've been found.
I've been lifted and been shut down.

I've been loved, and I've been heard.
I've been comforted without a word.

I've been seen and I've been cared for.
I've wanted less, and I've needed more.

I've held it together. I've busted to pieces.
I've told you my story. I've written my thesis.

I Am

Woke up this morning with a new outlook
No longer looking for the fairy tale from a book.
While I may be a mess, and a lot to handle.
I don't need prince charming, because I'm no damsel.

What I am is beautiful and strong.
I'm the best part of your favorite song.
I am the lighting that strikes, and makes art in the sand.
I am sweet and spicy and far from bland.

I am smart and classy and a little bit mean,
When I feel I'm being brushed off and unseen.
I am courageous and scared, wrapped up into one.
I'm a singer and dancer. I like to have fun.

I've been through a lot. My armor is thick.
I'm addicted to love. I don't move on quick.
I am timid at times and a mystery to most.
I am humble most days. I don't like to boast.

I like to laugh and I hate to cry.
I'll trust with my whole heart, 'til I catch you in a lie.
I'm a believer of all-in, I wear my heart on my sleeve.
I'm an emotional mess, when people choose to leave.

I'm a thinker and a writer.
I'm a lover, and I am a fighter.
I'm a foodie and a baker.
I'm an adventure risk taker.

I'm a couch potato and an outdoor fiend.
I'm direct as they come, if you know what I mean.
I can be soft spoken, but I like to be heard.
When I start to speak, I mean every word.

So this morning as I awoke, and sat up in my bed.
I silence the negative thoughts floating in my head.
So I threw off my covers and stood nice and tall.
Because while I may have stumbled, I refuse to fall.

Lasting Impact

You made a lasting impact.
From the very moment that we met.
Each new thing we learned together,
My heart won't soon forget.

You brought me out of my shell,
And showed me just who I could be.
I showed you all the hidden parts,
No one was brave enough to seek.

You taught me how to love myself,
And to dream the biggest dreams,
You make me laugh at every turn,
With all your smirks and memes.

You see me to my core,
And can read me like a book.
You know my every thought I have inside,
You know my every look.

We talk about the most random things,
No one understands our bond,
You will still be my favorite person,
Long after we're both gone.

You've been my person from the jump,
In every single way.
And you always come back around,
Even when I push you away.

I'm so glad that I have met you,
And that you're my best friend.
Because a life without you in it
Is not one I recommend.

Make My Heart See

It's been weeks since I've seen you.
Even more since I've felt your touch.
I want to say I'm moving on,
But I miss you too much.

Your towel still hangs on the rack,
Your toothbrush is still by the sink.
Your memories still float round my head,
So I write to process and think.

I feel so confused.
Trapped in a country song.
How did something so right,
End up so wrong?

The weeks that pass don't take your memory
with them,
Instead I see you everywhere.
Very few moments and places pass
Where I don't wish you were there.

I try to put on a brave face,
And tell my heart to listen to my head.
But the thoughts of you are everywhere,
So my heart wins out instead.

If I were able to listen to my own advice
I would know that this is wrong for me,
But instead your words play on repeat
My heart string's melody.

I still hold on to the hope
We can again trust one another.
But Your words say one thing,
And your actions quite another.

You say that you love me
And that I'm the best thing for you.
But then I'm ignored so long,
That I don't believe that it's true.

You say you just need some time.
And that you're healing.
I give you all that you ask for
Despite how I'm feeling.

I push my pain aside, to help you heal
Because the love I have is so deep
But the comfort is one sided
The price I'm paying is too steep.

So while I know it will take awhile
And I am not quite ready yet
It is time I start to process,
Move on, and forget.

It's time I start listening to my head
And stop following my heart
Because while I gave you the whole thing
You just keep ripping it apart.

So I'm picking up the pieces
And taking my pride along with me
I deserve more than what you give
I just have to make my heart see.

I'm Learning

I'm learning how to let go
But the healing I need will be slow.

I keep moving forward, taking it one day at a time.
But there is no quick fix for this heart of mine.

I'm learning how to love myself again.
Finding the love I need from within.

I'm learning to accept there are things I can't change,
But that my personality is not what needed to be rearranged.

I'm learning that some people are here only for a season,
And that when things don't work out, there is a reason.

I'm learning that sometimes I give too much and accept too little.
I'm learning that I can't go the whole way, but need to meet them in the middle.

I'm learning that my heart and my head need to be in sync.
And that there are times where I really need to stop and think.

I need to stop ignoring the red flags because my love goggles are on.
I need to learn when people leave, to make them stay gone.

I'm learning second and third chances aren't worth this pain.
I shouldn't be left with so many questions bouncing around my brain.

I'm learning that I should pay attention to actions more than words.
And that I shouldn't sweep it under the rug and should talk out my concerns.

I'm learning that the best is yet to come, I just need to wait.
I'm learning that I can't keep being caught on these gaslighter's bait.

Yes I am learning how to let go,
But be patient as this process will be slow.

Smile Through the Trial

While the smile may be fake,
The sentiment is real.
I am trying to be happy,
While I process how I feel.

Pain is often swift,
But the recovery takes a while.
So I'm doing the best I can,
To deal with it and smile.

So if you see a smile planted firmly on my face,
Know that I am trying,
And that while you see a smile,
My insides may be crying.

I am doing the best I can
To make it through the day,
And hope that you are kind,
When a smile is all I "say".

Each day I get a little closer
And I cry a little less.
But even on the days I've faltered,
I've truly done my best.

Of course I still grieve,
And don't understand all that I feel,
But I hope that when the crying stops,
I can truly start to heal.

Now I know this will be a process,
And that there will still be pain inside,
But I pray the tears remain at bay,
And my emotions don't all collide.

I am ready for the fight
That will rage inside of me,
But I hope that I tame it enough
That outsiders cannot see.

While the smile may be fake,
The sentiment is real.
I am trying to be happy,
While I process how I feel.

Moving On

My heart may be a little calloused,
My temperament a little meak.
BUt I am learning a little more each day,
To use my voice and speak.

I don't know what it is I want,
But I am finding what I don't.
I want someone who will stick around,
Because I've found most won't

I don't want someone who is good with words,
But poor in following through.
I don't want someone who can't commit,
Let's try out something new.

I don't want to feel alone,
When you're standing by my side.
I don't want to feel the same
As I did, each time that I cried.

I don't want to hold onto this pain, I am ready to let it go.
I want to find someone who sees me,
When I don't let my feelings show.

I don't want to stay in this cycle,
Of pain and misery.
I want to find someone who loves the worst parts,
The ones I don't let others see.

I don't want to keep thinking of the past,
I want to leave it there.
I want to show the people I loves,
Just how much I truly care.

I don't want to hide myself anymore,
I want those days to be gone.
Looking toward a new horizon,
Embracing a new Dawn.

Printed in the USA
CPSIA information can be obtained
at www.ICGtesting.com
LVHW021213110924
790748LV00017B/736